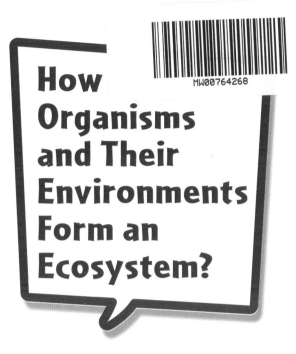

How Organisms and Their Environments Form an Ecosystem?

 HOUGHTON MIFFLIN HARCOURT

PHOTOGRAPHY CREDITS: COVER ©Radius Images/Corbis; 3 (b) ©William Leaman/Alamy Images; 5 (tr) ©Gilles DeCruyenaere/Shutterstock; 7 (b) ©Richard Wear/Design Pics/Corbis; 9 (t) ©Rimantas Abromas/Shutterstock; 12 (b) ©2009fotofriends/Shutterstock; 13 (t) ©Anders Blomqvist/Lonely Planet Images/Getty Images; 16 (b) ©Noel Hendrickson/Digital Vision/Getty Images; 17 (t) ©Radius Images/Corbis; 17 (inset) ©Jeff Rotman/Science Source/ Photo Researchers, Inc.; 18 (r) ©Black Rock Digital/Shutterstock; 19 (b) ©Karl Weatherly/Photodisc/Getty Images; 20 (tr) ©Photo Researchers/Getty Images; 21 (cr) ©Guenter Fischer/Imagebroker/Alamy Images

Printed in Mexico

ISBN: 978-0-544-07344-9

8 9 10 0908 21 20 19 18 17

4500670288   A B C D E F G

Be an Active Reader!

Look for each word in yellow along with its meaning.

environment	photosynthesis	decomposer
ecosystem	producer	food web
habitat	consumer	succession
niche	food chain	extinction

Underlined sentences answer the questions.

Where do organisms live?

What living things make up an ecosystem?

How do plants get energy to live?

How does energy move in an ecosystem?

How does energy move in a food web?

How can environmental changes affect organisms?

How does an ecosystem go through succession?

How can environmental changes help or hurt an ecosystem?

How do invasive species affect an ecosystem?

What happens to some organisms on Earth?

Where do organisms live?

You can see many different plants and animals in a forest. Birds nest in the trees. Squirrels dig for nuts. Plants grow from healthy soil. All of the plants and animals use the rain that falls from the sky. An environment is all the living and nonliving things that surround and affect an organism. The nonliving parts of an environment include soil, water, and rocks. The nonliving parts are called abiotic. The living parts, such as plants and animals, are called biotic parts.

An environment and all the organisms living in it are called an ecosystem. Organisms live in ecosystems where they can meet their needs and survive.

A forest is one kind of ecosystem.

What living things make up an ecosystem?

Take a close look at the forest ecosystem. You will notice different groups of living things. You may notice blue jays, raccoons, owls, and insects. You may see plants such as ferns and oak trees. A group of organisms of the same species in an ecosystem is called a population. All of the maple trees in one forest are a population. All of the earthworms in the forest are also a population.

Each organism in an ecosystem depends on other organisms. An ecosystem with many populations is diverse. Most of Earth's diverse ecosystems are close to the equator.

All of the populations that live and interact with each other in an ecosystem are called a community. The populations include animal populations and plant populations. Many animals in a community compete for food. The community outside your schoolyard is a part of an ecosystem.

Organisms can survive only where their needs are met. A habitat is a place where an organism lives within an ecosystem. Without a habitat, an organism would not have the resources it needs to live. For example, prairie dogs must live in grassland areas. They could not survive in a desert habitat.

A niche is an organism's complete role, or function, in its ecosystem. A niche includes the kinds of foods

This monarch caterpillar eats only milkweed. The monarch has a narrow niche.

the organism eats and the climate it needs in order to thrive. It even includes the way the organism obtains and eats its food. If certain organisms share a niche in an ecosystem, they have to compete for the same resources.

A niche can be narrow or broad. Animals that eat only a small number of specific foods have a narrow niche. Animals with a broad niche eat a wide variety of foods.

How do plants get energy to live?

Animals get their energy from eating organisms in their ecosystem. Plants make their own food through a process called photosynthesis. The food gives them the energy they need to survive.

For photosynthesis to occur, water, sunlight, and a gas called carbon dioxide are needed. Water from soil enters the plant's roots. Carbon dioxide enters tiny holes in the plant's leaves. Chlorophyll is a green pigment in plants. It allows a plant cell to take in sunlight to make food. The energy from sunlight changes the water and carbon dioxide into sugar. The plant uses the sugar to live. The plant also makes a gas called oxygen. The oxygen is released into the air as waste.

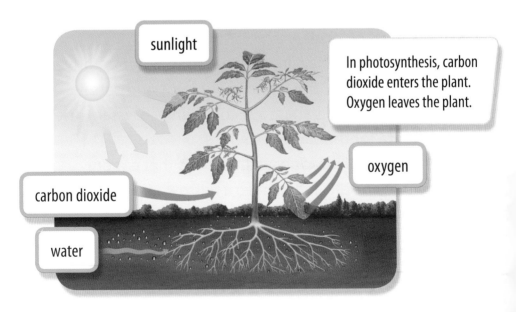

sunlight

In photosynthesis, carbon dioxide enters the plant. Oxygen leaves the plant.

oxygen

carbon dioxide

water

The carbon dioxide–oxygen cycle is a natural cycle in Earth's atmosphere. Carbon dioxide and oxygen move from the atmosphere to living things and back again.

Where do plants get the carbon dioxide they need for photosynthesis? They get it from animals! How? Animals get the oxygen they need from the air they breathe into their lungs. They produce carbon dioxide as waste. It moves from the lungs to the animal's nose or mouth and then out of the animal's body. Animals breathe out the carbon dioxide that plants need to live. The carbon dioxide–oxygen cycle is an example of how plants and animals in an ecosystem depend on each other.

Plants and animals in an ecosystem are part of the carbon dioxide–oxygen cycle.

How does energy move in an ecosystem?

A plant is called a producer because it makes, or produces, its own food. Each animal in an ecosystem is called a consumer. Consumers get energy from eating, or consuming, living things. Consumers that eat only plants are called herbivores. Consumers that eat only animals are called carnivores. Omnivores eat both plants and animals.

After a plant gets energy from sunlight, the energy is passed along. As an animal eats a plant, the energy from the plant passes to the animal. Then that animal may be eaten by another animal. The energy is passed on again.

The transfer of energy between organisms in an ecosystem is called a food chain. A food chain is used to tell the order in which the energy flows. All food chains start with the sun. Energy passes from the sun to producers.

sun

producer

first-level consumer

second-level consumer

third-level consumer

A food chain shows how energy passes from producer to consumer.

Fungi are one kind of decomposer. Like bacteria, they return nutrients to soil.

Then producers eat consumers. For example, grasses grow, using sunlight to produce food. A rabbit eats the grasses, and some of the energy flows to the rabbit. The rabbit is a first-level consumer. Energy is passed to a fox when it eats the rabbit. The fox is a second-level consumer.

Next, a golden eagle eats the fox. The energy goes from the fox to the eagle. The golden eagle is a third-level consumer.

Next in the food chain are the decomposers. A decomposer breaks down the remains of dead organisms. Bacteria and fungi are examples of decomposers. In the food chain described here, bacteria will return nutrients that were part of the organism to the soil.

How does energy move in a food web?

A food chain shows how energy moves through an ecosystem. Hundreds of different organisms eat many different foods. The rabbit eats many kinds of plants. The rattlesnake and hawk each eat many kinds of animals. A group of food chains that overlap is called a food web. Every kind of ecosystem has food chains and food webs.

This food web shows how animals get energy from many different sources. Choose an animal. Explain what the animal eats. What eats the animal?

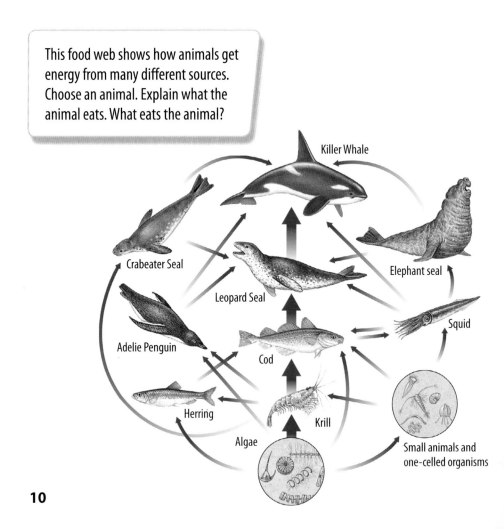

Killer Whale

Crabeater Seal

Leopard Seal

Elephant seal

Adelie Penguin

Squid

Cod

Herring

Krill

Algae

Small animals and one-celled organisms

What if one kind of organism in the web is removed? Relationships between organisms in the web change. If the rattlesnake is removed from the web, this takes away one of the hawk's food sources. The hawk might not be able to find enough food to stay alive.

An energy pyramid is a diagram that shows the energy available at each level in a food chain. More energy and more organisms are at the bottom of the pyramid. Less energy and fewer organisms are at the top.

When an animal eats an organism, 90% of the energy is used to keep the animal alive. Only 10% can be passed to the organism that eats it. The first-level consumers eat many plants to get the energy to live. There are fewer second-level consumers because they have less energy available to them. As you continue up the energy pyramid, less energy is passed to the higher-level consumers.

The wolf is at the top of the pyramid. It has the least amount of the sun's energy available to it.

How can environmental changes affect organisms?

Environments are changing all the time. Some changes are very slow. You can barely see these changes happening. Erosion is the process of moving Earth materials from one place to another. Erosion often happens very slowly. A mountaintop may wear away over a long period of time. Wind and rain move the rock and soil to new places. The top of the mountain may become smaller and reshape over time.

Erosion can affect the habitat of the organisms that live on the mountaintop. The plants have a smaller area in which to grow. The animals have a smaller area in which to move around and look for food. In order to survive, the organisms must change, or they must be able to move to a new environment.

Erosion can break down a mountaintop. This change leaves less room for plants to grow and animals to live.

A mudslide can quickly change an ecosystem.

Organisms don't always have time to adapt to quick changes in their ecosystem. For example, many plants cannot survive a flood because it happens quickly.

Mudslides are also fast changes. Soil and rocks may quickly slide from a higher area to a lower area. Trees may be part of these mudslides, too. Thousands of organisms may be in the way of the heavy debris. The debris can move the organisms and their homes. The debris can also destroy habitats and food supplies.

A quick change like a mudslide can also cause food supplies to change. Some animals may not be able to move to another area to find what they need to live.

How does an ecosystem go through succession?

Ecosystems can recover after big changes. Succession is a gradual change in the kinds of organisms in an ecosystem. Succession may occur after a fast change, such as a volcanic eruption. The entire ground may be covered in ash. Often, only bare rock is left. Tiny organisms such as moss or lichen may grow on the rock. Over time, soil is created when the rock breaks down. Plants grow in the soil. Small animals come to feed on the plants. In time, the plants die. Their remains decay and add nutrients to the soil.

These changes are so slow that we do not even notice them happening. Over generations, bushes grow and larger animals move to the area. Trees grow and are home to many animals. Succession that starts from bare rock is called primary succession.

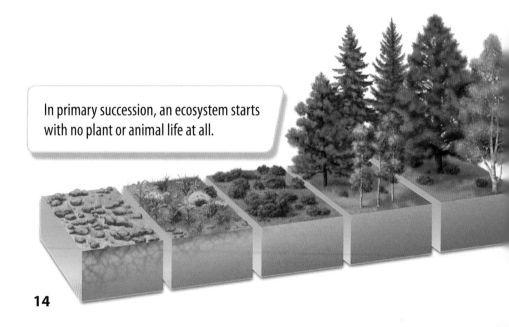

In primary succession, an ecosystem starts with no plant or animal life at all.

Some changes do not destroy the soil in an ecosystem. Forest fires can cause huge changes. However, the soil is still present. Succession that starts from soil is called secondary succession. This kind of succession is faster than primary succession.

Seeds and roots may grow in the soil soon after the fire. Plants such as shrubs and grass grow. They become food sources for many living things. Larger plants then take hold. The new ecosystem may become dense with life.

In secondary succession, it may take only a few years for trees to reappear after a forest fire.

How can environmental changes help or hurt an ecosystem?

Not all forest fires destroy an ecosystem. Lightning can strike and cause a forest fire. Heat from the fire causes pine cones high in trees to open up. The cones release seeds that are inside them. The seeds fall to the ground. In time, the seeds may grow into new trees.

Forest fires might also help to reduce the number of harmful insects in an area. Too many large trees in an area can keep sunlight from reaching smaller plants. The fires may prevent large trees from taking over the area.

Forest fires can be destructive. But they can be helpful to forest ecosystems in some ways.

coral reef damaged by coral bleaching

healthy coral reef

Coral reefs are damaged when water becomes too warm or too cold.

Some changes within an ecosystem can be very harmful. For example, a coral reef is an important ocean habitat. Coral is made of tiny organisms called polyps. The polyps grow and spread to large areas. Many fish and other species depend on a reef for shelter. Algae live in the coral and are responsible for the variety of colors of some coral. The algae make food that the coral uses. Many marine animals then eat the coral.

Some coral reefs are becoming damaged. When the water gets too warm or too cold, the coral releases the algae. The coral looks white, or bleached, without the algae. The coral also no longer has the food the algae provided.

How do invasive species affect an ecosystem?

Most animals have natural predators. The predators keep the population of those animals from getting too large. But what happens when a species from another place is introduced into an ecosystem? An invasive species is one that invades, or takes over, a place. The invasive species can take over because it has no natural predators in an ecosystem. Invasive species take the food supply from native species in the area. Invasive plants compete for space in an ecosystem. They take hold in the ground and crowd out other plants. Invasive plants may reproduce quickly. They can reduce or destroy populations of native plants.

Kudzu is a plant from Asia. It was brought into the United States to help control soil erosion. Kudzu competes for space with all of the other plants around it.

Invasive species are brought to new ecosystems in different ways. People may put a plant from another area of the world into their garden. They may let a pet or other animal loose into a new environment. Birds can introduce invasive species. Birds may carry plant seeds to new places.

Lake trout is an invasive species that has damaged the ecosystem of Yellowstone National Park. A lake trout appeared in the area. The trout has been slowly taking over the ecosystem. It takes the food of the Yellowstone cutthroat trout, which is endangered, or close to dying out. The lake trout has no natural predators in the Yellowstone ecosystem. The population grows quickly. Scientists find it challenging to help the ecosystem return to balance.

The invasive lake trout competes for resources with the endangered cutthroat trout.

What happens to some organisms on Earth?

Some ecosystem changes cannot be repaired. When a plant or animal species no longer exists anywhere on Earth, extinction has occurred. Extinction can happen for many reasons. The organism may become unable to compete for resources. This causes the organism to die off faster than it can reproduce.

The passenger pigeon became extinct in 1914.

People can play a role in the extinction of some animals. People may hunt or fish in an area too much. We may also build homes or roads where organisms live.

Natural changes to ecosystems can cause extinctions, too. Massive volcanoes may erupt and send ash into the air. Large asteroids may hit Earth. These events are rare, but they can change Earth's climate. Climate change can cause many species to become extinct in a short amount of time.

People can help keep some plants and animals from becoming extinct. Scientists make people aware of which species are close to dying out. People can help to protect the habitats of these organisms.

People can also help keep ecosystems healthy. This may mean limiting the areas where people build. It may mean not hunting or fishing for some species. These actions can help the communities in ecosystems stay balanced.

Scientists learn about relationships in ecosystems. The scientists do this by studying how organisms interact with the living and nonliving parts of their environment. What scientists learn can help keep human activities from harming ecosystems.

The Texas star cactus is an endangered plant species. Loss of habitat and over-harvesting by cactus collectors have threatened its survival in the wild. It is now a protected species in Texas.

Model a Food Web

Work with a partner. Choose an ecosystem, and research the interactions between plants and animals in that ecosystem. Make a model of a food web, including as many organisms as you can. Use arrows to connect the pictures or models of each plant or animal.

Make a Poster

Choose an ecosystem that interests you. Make a poster that explains the importance of protecting that ecosystem and the organisms that live in it. The poster should include ways that people can help the ecosystem and prevent organisms from becoming extinct.

Glossary

consumer [kuhn·SOOM·er] A living thing that cannot make its own food and must eat other living things. *A consumer may eat plants or other animals.*

decomposer [dee·kuhm·POH·ser] A living thing that gets energy by breaking down dead organisms and animal wastes into simpler substances. *Bacteria are a kind of decomposer.*

ecosystem [EE·koh·sis·tuhm] A community of organisms and the environment in which they live. *An ecosystem may have many plants and animals in it.*

environment [en·VY·ruhn·muhnt] All the living and nonliving things that surround and affect an organism. *The environment around you includes rocks, water, and living things.*

extinction [ek·STINGK·shuhn] A plant or an animal species that is no longer living or existing. *Many endangered animals are close to extinction.*

food chain [FOOD CHAYN] The transfer of food energy between organisms in an ecosystem. *A food chain can be on land or in water.*

food web [FOOD WEB] A group of food chains that overlap. *Many organisms are part of a food web.*

habitat [HAB·i·tat] The place where an organism lives and can find everything it needs to survive. *An ocean habitat is home to many fish.*

niche [NICH] The role a plant or animal plays in its habitat. *Some animals have a narrow niche because they eat only a few kinds of food.*

photosynthesis [foh·toh·SIN·thuh·sis] The process that plants use to make their own food. *A plant makes its own food through the process of photosynthesis.*

producer [pruh·DOOS·er] A living thing, such as a plant, that can make its own food. *Every plant is a producer.*

succession [suhk·SESH·uhn] A gradual change of the kinds of organisms in an ecosystem. *Succession may occur after a forest fire.*